T0058946

BASIC BLUES ETUDES
IN ALL TWELVE KEYS by Jordon Ruwe

Table of Contents

ISBN 0-7935-9599-1

Houston
PUBLISHING, INC.

EXCLUSIVELY DISTRIBUTED BY

HAL•LEONARD®
CORPORATION

7777 W. BLUEMOUND RD. P.O. BOX 13819 MILWAUKEE, WI 53213

Visit Hal Leonard Online at
www.halleonard.com

Introduction

The blues are an integral part of our society. Jazz, Rock, Rhythm and Blues could not have become what they are today without this great form of music. Most blues are twelve bars in length. There are some twelve bar blues with a bridge and some rare cases of 8 bar blues. This book is a basic 12 bar blues using only 3 chords. All the chords that are being used are called dominant seventh chords.

All chords are derived from scale systems. The basic system that the dominant seventh chord comes from is the fifth step of a major scale. The mode title of the fifth step is called Mixolydian mode. All the steps of the major scale have modal names. Knowing the scale systems that best fit each chord helps the player in choosing the better notes for their solos or writing.

Playing through all the etudes in this book will help the player develop facility through the keys. If you have not played the blues before, this book should help you to develop a closer feeling for the basic twelve bar blues.

If you wish to continue your blues journey, I have written two other books on the blues with more complex changes. They are: *Major Blues in All Twelve Keys* and *Minor Blues in All Twelve Keys*.

Blues Etude in the Key of G

Blues Etude in the Key of C

Blues Etude in the Key of F

Blues Etude in the Key of Bb

Blues Etude in the Key of Eb

Blues Etude in the Key of Ab

Blues Etude in the Key of Db

Blues Etude in the Key of F#

Blues Etude in the Key of B

Blues Etude in the Key of E

Blues Etude in the Key of A

Blues Etude in the Key of D

Excerpt from the Key of G
All Keys

Excerpt from the Key of G
All Keys

Excerpt from the Key of B
All Keys

Excerpt from the Key of B
All Keys

This page has been left blank intentionally.

Excerpt from the Key of F
All Keys

Excerpt from the Key of F
All Keys

This page has been left blank intentionally.

Excerpt from the Key of Db
All Keys

Excerpt from the Key of Db
All Keys

This page has been left blank intentionally.

Excerpt from the Key of D
All Keys

45

Excerpt from the Key of Eb
All Keys

Excerpt from the Key of A
All Keys

Excerpt from the Key of F#
All Keys

V7 b9 Moving Up by Minor Thirds

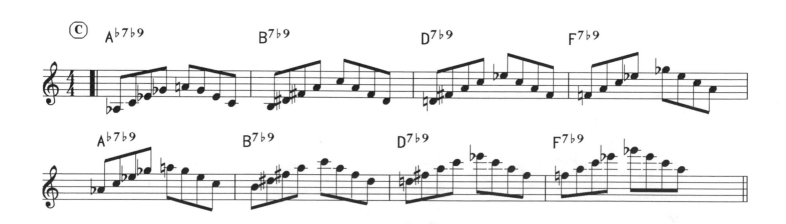

V7 b9 Moving Down by Minor Thirds

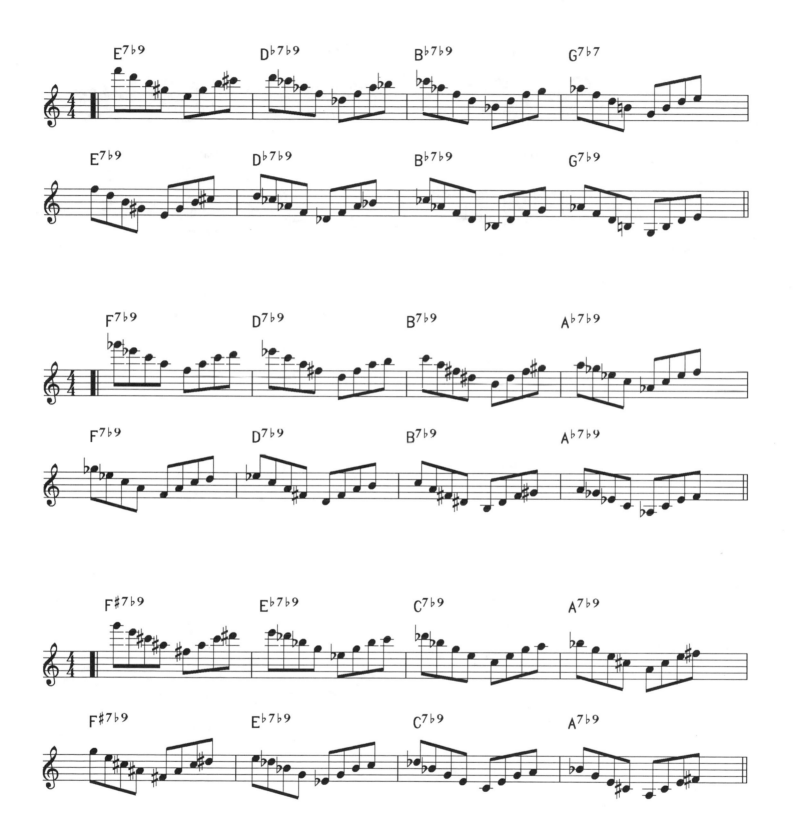

ii V7 Cycle of Fourths

II⁷ V⁷ I Jazz Riff in all Keys

54

ii V7 I Exercise in All Keys

Dominant Sevenths Moving Down by Whole Steps

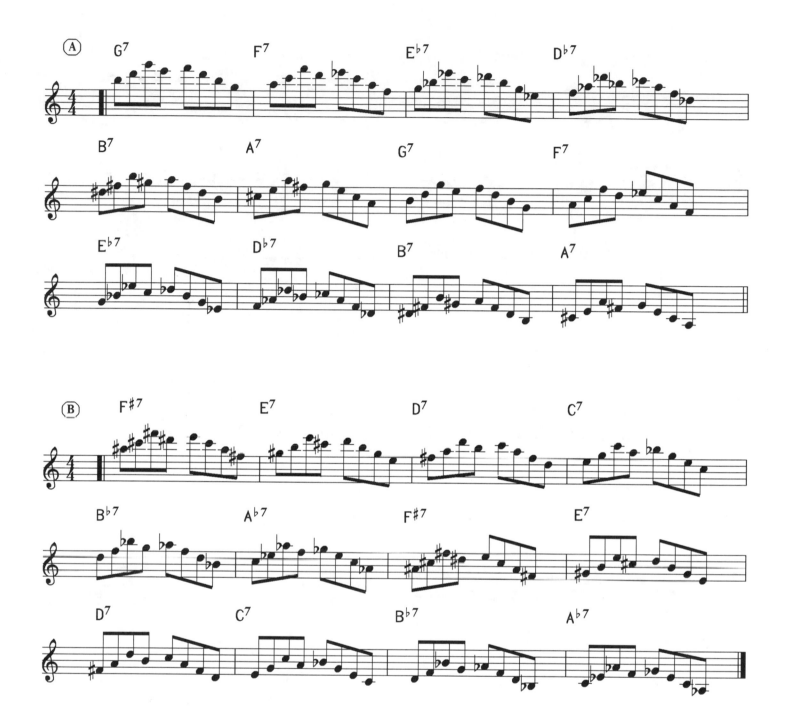

56

Diminished Exercise

Exercise Moving Down by Whole Steps

Transposing Exercise

Transpose the following blues in all keys after playing through this book. If you need to write it our, feel free to do so.

About the Author

Jordon Ruwe played with the great blues legend "Guitar Shorty" (who can be seen in the March 1995 issue of *Downbeat Magazine*). It was here that he received his "training" in learning the many types of blues forms, including the basic blues.

Jordon studied with many great woodwind artists including saxophone with Joseph Allard and Art Pepper, flute with Frank Horsfall, clarinet with Tom Solberg, and theory with Dr. Mary Elisabeth Duncan. He has played with Larry Coryell, Diane Schuur, Jay Thomas, David Friesen, Denny Goodhue, and many other notables. The popularity of his books, *Technical Exercises for the Intermediate to Professional Jazz Musician, Vital Elements for the Jazz Flutist, Minor Blues Tunes in All Twelve Keys,* and *Major Blues Tunes in All Twelve Keys* attest to his ability to provide useful instructional material for the aspiring musician.